Michael M. Dediu

World Constitution

WITH QUESTIONS & ANSWERS

Moving from many obsolete
constitutions to the much better
Constitution of the World

DERC Publishing House

Nashua, New Hampshire, U. S. A.

Published and printed in the
United States of America
On the Great Seal of the United States are included:
E Pluribus Unum (Out of many, one)
Annuit Coeptis (He has approved of the undertakings)
Novus Ordo Seclorum (New order of the ages)

Library of Congress Control Number: 2020916609

Dediu, Michael M.

World Constitution with Questions & Answers
Moving from many obsolete constitutions to the much better
Constitution of the World

ISBN-13: 978-1-950999-20-0

MSG0455679_DJi4EFO52MvlS7eb3x2W
MSG0456446_OGSdfE89250rtN23EwYf
1-9264593711
1-497WEDK
26PUERKF

Preface

There are many fundamental questions that all human beings are called to answer. The most important philosophers, including Socrates, Plato, Aristotle, Descartes, and Kant, always asked profound questions, and gave eternal answers. The Constitution of the World certainly encourages questions, and offers in advance some direct and accurate answers – all these questions and answers will help the World Constitution to be better understood, and easier to implement by the people.

There are many questions, from "What is the objective of this Constitution?" and "What is the first priority?", to "Who can declare war?" and "Will everybody have a job?", all with precise responses, based on The Constitution of the World.

This book discusses over 65 questions, giving complete responses, emphasizing on the new ideas from the Constitution of the World, which will create the conditions for a peaceful, free and prosperous new country, Peaceful Terra.

The future begins to take shape in front of our eyes, and it is astonishingly beautiful!

Michael M. Dediu, Ph. D.

Nashua, New Hampshire, U. S. A., 12 September 2020

USA, UC Berkeley (1868, motto Fiat lux), from Campanile (1914, 94 m) looking north-northwest: Mathematics Dep. and Economics Dep. (right middle), Civil Engineering Dep. (next back), Nanofabrication Lab. (next back), Transportation Inst. (center left), Earth Sciences and Map Library and Seismological Lab (next left), Graduate School of Journalism (next back), Center for Developing Economies (next right), Memorial Glade (green center left).

Table of Contents

Italy, Udine: 3 Nov 2009, on Via Nicolo Lionello, just southwest of Loggia del Lionello, looking east to the southwest façade of the Palazzo di Comune di Udine (City Hall).

The Constitution of the World

Question 1. What is the objective of this Constitution?

Response 1. The objective is simply to help all the people on Earth to live better, peacefully, free, healthy, and prosperous.

More precisely, the Constitution starts with 7 details about its objectives in Proposition 1:

Proposition 1. We, the People of the World

We, the People on this Earth, in order to

1.1 - completely eliminate war and any type of conflicts,

1.2 - have a peaceful and harmonious world,

1.3 - have freedom, dignity, good families and respect,

1.4 - have good health and good education,

1.5 - have a friendly atmosphere and prosperity,

1.6 – have the safety and wellbeing of all the people in the world as the highest priority,

1.7 – use the best peaceful results, experience and knowledge of all current countries,

establish this Constitution of the World.

Italy, Venezia - In the middle of the west façade of the Basilica di San Marco, we see the central bronze-fashioned door, in a round-arched portal, encircled by polychrome marble columns. Above this door there are three round bas-relief cycles of Romanesque art. A Japanese couple, with their Japanese photographer, make their wedding photographs in this most beautiful place.

Question 2. What is the first priority?

Response 2. Peace is the first priority – without peace not much can be done.

Proposition 2 has the title Peaceful Terra.

France, Paris, mannequins representing Gustave Eiffel (right, 57 years old) talking in 1889 to Thomas Edison (left, 42 years old) in Eiffel's apartment in Tour Eiffel (1889, 324 m).

Japan, the entrance to a building with a teaching auditorium, 100 m west from the north-east entrance of the Inzai campus of Tokyo Denki University (a private university founded in 1907, and chartered as a university in 1949), 35 km north-east of Tokyo Imperial Palace, 24 km west of Narita International Airport.

Question 3. How many countries?

Response 3. Just one beautiful country - Peaceful Terra.

Point 2.1 from Proposition 2 gives some details:
All the people of the world will be proud citizens of only one country, called Peaceful Terra, with total area of over 509 M km^2, and land area over 148 M km^2.

Being just one country, there are no borders:

4.1 - In Peaceful Terra there are no borders.

UK, London, from the Westminster Bridge (1862) looking southwest to the southern part of Palace of Westminster (1016, 1870, right), a tall residential building (center left) near Millbank Millennium Pier, and The Tower (left, condominium complex, on Nine Elms Lane).

Question 4. How many rules will be in this Peaceful Terra?

Response 4. Not too many – the point 2.2 from Proposition 2 explains:

2.2 - All the rules – not more than 2,000, on maximum 1,000 pages - on our Earth will be established by the people and their elected Advisers.

Proposition 36. Limited number of rules

36.1 - All rules proposed by Advisers must be approved by their 5 assistants (doctors, mathematicians, CEOs, engineers and teachers), and for any new rule over 2,000 basic rules (each rule on at most half a page, total 1,000 pages), at least on old rule must be eliminated.

36.2 - All the rules can be changed or eliminated when a majority of the people or their Advisors agree, but some fundamental peace and order rules will remain.

Question 5. How will this Peaceful Terra be administrated?

Response 5. Being a very big country, will be divided in 10 simple regions - Proposition 3 presents the details:

Proposition 3. Ten Simple and Friendly Regions

3.1 - For easier administration, Peaceful Terra will be only administratively divided in 10 simple and friendly regions of around 770 M people each, called R0, R1,…, R9, which will be delimited by meridians (or line of longitudes), with the assistance of the United Nations.

Australia: In Sydney (1788, 5 M people), from the Royal Botanic Gardens looking to the southeast side of the harbourfront Sydney Opera House (1959-1973, 183 m by 120 m by 65 m height, total seating capacity 5738)) and the Sydney Harbour Bridge (1932, left).

Question 6. Where will the capital of this Peaceful Terra be?

Response 6. Everywhere! Because the capitals tend to become huge bureaucracies, with lots of people trying to be there, without much usefulness, Peaceful Terra will have moving capitals, to benefit everybody. More details are given in point 3.2 of the Proposition 3:

3.2 - Each region will have a pair of capitals plus an outside city, for better and more homogenous management (all will change every year; more details are in the annex book "World with One Country & its Ten Friendly Regions - Moving from 195 disagreeing countries, to 1 country with 10 collaborating regions"). For example, the first implementation will be:
R0 between meridians 0 and 15^0 E, capitals: Bern (Switzerland), Libreville (Gabon), and Oxford (UK).
R1: 15^0 E - 30^0 E, Warsaw (Poland), Pretoria (South Africa) and Miami (FL, USA).
R2: 30^0 E - 45^0 E, Moscow (Russia), Cairo (Egypt), and Grenoble (France).
R3: 45^0 E - 75^0 E, Astana (Kazakhstan), Karachi (Pakistan), and Montpellier (France).
R4: 75^0 E - 85^0 E, New Delhi (India), Novosibirsk (Russia), and Magdeburg (Germany).
R5: 85^0 E - 100^0 E, Krasnoyarsk (Russia), Urumqi (China), and Avignon (France).
R6: 100^0 E - 115^0 E, Jakarta (Indonesia), Beijing (China), and Neuchâtel (Switzerland).
R7: 115^0 E - 180^0, Tokyo (Japan), Sydney (Australia), and Malmö (Sweden).
R8: 180^0 - 70^0 Washington (USA), Mexico City (Mexico), and Bellinzona (Switzerland).
R9: 70^0 W – 0 Halifax (Canada), Brasilia (Brazil), and Biel (Switzerland).

UK, On Gagarin (First Man in Space) Terrace, on the southwest part of the South Building (1899) of the Royal Observatory Greenwich (1676), looking northeast to the south part of the west side (right), the west part of the south side (left), and to the statue of Yuri Gagarin (1934-1968, Russian cosmonaut, the first man to journey into space, with Vostok spacecraft, which completed an orbit (1h 48') of the Earth on 12 April 1961. Resting place: Kremlin Wall Necropolis).

There are many big differences between the populations of different regions, in the first implementation, but points 4.3, 4.4 and 4.5 explain:

4.3 - In the first implementation presented in Proposition 3, there are many big differences between the populations of different regions, and then between the populations of different sub-regions, but this is just the first implementation, which needs to be quickly put in place, and then, very easily, the delimitations will be moved a few kilometers east or west, to reach a balanced population.

4.4 - Because all the people are in the same country, it is normal to modify a little its regions, for better administration, to make everybody happy.

4.5 - It is well understood that there will be some difficulties in the beginning, like in all beginnings, but with calm, patience, perseverance and hard work, the things will improve fast, and all the people will enjoy a better life.

USA: Plymouth (1620, 60 km southeast of Boston) – Plymouth Rock with the year 1620, when the first ship Mayflower arrived in America.

In Malmö, southwest of Sweden, taking the boat from Malmö to Köpenhamn (Copenhagen, Denmark, 25 km northwest of Malmö).

Question 7. How many subdivisions will be in each Region?

Response 7. Ten – more details are in point 3.2 of Proposition 3:

3.2. Each of the 10 regions will be divided by meridians in 10 sub-regions S00, , S99, each with about 77 M people.

Then each of the 100 sub-regions will be divided in 10 districts:

3.3. Each of the 100 sub-regions will be divided in 10 districts D000, D001, , D999, each with about 7.7 M people, and each of the districts will have their current small and big cities.

All these delimitations between regions, as well as between sub-regions, will be flexible:

4.2 - There will be just simple administrative delimitations, and all these delimitations between regions, as well as between sub-regions, will be flexible – they will be changed after each census (5 years), for maintaining a balanced number of people in all regions (around 770 M) and sub-regions (around 77 M).

Question 8. Why are the meridians used for divisions?

Response 8: Meridians are easy to use, impartial, helpful for people with telework – more details in point 3.4:

3.4. Having telework, many people will have a northern residence and a southern residence, seasonally moving from one to the other, to avoid extreme cold or heat, and having the same hour.

UK: On Newington Butts St., looking northwest to Metropolitan Tabernacle (1650, left) and London College of Communication.

Question 9. What is the status of the oceans?

Response 9: All the oceans will belong to some of the regions – details in 3.5:

3.5. All the oceans will belong to some of the regions defined above, therefore will be maintained by those regions, to be free of any piracy or other bad activity – World Police will help when necessary.

USA, Boston: 3 Dec 2009, from Avenue Louis Pasteur (1822-1895, French microbiologist), Boston Public Latin School (1635, Schola Latina Bostoniensis, the oldest and the first public exam school in the US).

UK, London, from the Shard (2012, 309 m, observatory at 244 m), looking east to the Tower Bridge (1886-1894, combined bascule and suspension turreted bridge over River Thames (flowing from west (left) to east (right)), between London boroughs Tower Hamlets (north – left up) and Southwark (south – right), length 244 m, height 65 m, longest span 82 m, clearance 8 m (closed), 42 m (open)), City Hall (2002, height 45 m, center right round, for the Greater London Authority: Mayor of London and the London Assembly)

Question 10. How the World Government looks like?

Response 10: Peaceful Terra, with its family of over 7.7 B people, will have four levels of world management – the first two levels are described in points 5.1, 5.2 and 5.3:

5.1. The family of over 7. 7 B people from Peaceful Terra will have four levels of world management; at the local level, if needed, it could be one or two more levels of local managers (mayors, town managers, county managers – all levels of management must be friendly, helpful, fast, polite, modest and smart):

5.2. Level 1 Management: 1,000 L1 friendly managers, for the 1,000 districts, who will supervise and assist the mayors and town managers from their district, for a total of about 7,700,000 people in each district. Each of the 1,000 L1 friendly managers will be located in a central city from their districts – they could be the mayors of those cities, but with new responsibilities for the whole district.

5.3. Level 2 Management: 100 L2 friendly managers, for the 100 sub-regions, who will supervise and assist the 10 L1 managers of the 10 districts of each sub-region, for a total of about 77,000,000 people for each sub-region. These 100 L2 friendly managers will move each month between the two capitals of each of the 100 sub-regions.

Oxford: From Merton Str., looking southeast to the north (left) and west (right) facades of Merton College Chapel (1294, 1425, 1451, the church of Merton College (1264, the third oldest in Oxford)); there were plans to extend this church to the west (right), but the land was leased in 1517 to Bishop Richard Foxe (1448-1528), who founded Corpus Christy College (1517), next door (west) to Merton.

Question 11. What are the two capitals for each sub-region?

Response 11: In the beginning these capitals will be:

In Region R0: from Paris (France) to N'Djamena (Chad)

- The sub-region R00 will have the capitals Paris (France) and Niamey (Niger) – assistance from Magdeburg (Germany).
- The sub-region R01 will have the capitals Brussels (Belgium) and Porto-Novo (Benin) - assistance from Toronto (Canada).
- The sub-region R02 will have the capitals Amsterdam (Netherlands) and Algiers (Algeria) - assistance from Graz (Austria).
- The sub-region R03 will have the capitals Luxembourg (Luxembourg) and Sao Tome (Sao Tome and Principe) - assistance from Adelaide (Australia).
- The sub-region R04 will have the capitals of Abuja (Nigeria) and Bochum (Germany) - assistance from Nikko (Japan).
- The sub-region R05 will have the capitals Malabo (Equatorial Guinea), and Zürich (Switzerland) - assistance from Leeds (UK).
- The sub-region R06 will have the capitals Oslo (Norway) and Tunis (Tunisia) - assistance from Sheffield (UK).
- The sub-region R07 will have the capitals Roma (Italy) and Luanda (Angola) - assistance from Yamagata (Japan).
- The sub-region R08 will have the capitals in Berlin (Germany) and Tripoli (Libya) - assistance from New York (USA).
- The sub-region R09 will have the capitals Prague (Czech Republic) and N'Djamena (Chad) - assistance from Brisbane (Australia).

Australia: On the Sydney Harbour Bridge (1932, 134 m height (the tallest in the world), length 1,149 m, width 49 m, 49 m above water), from car, on the sign: "For city streets follow lane colors below"

USA: New York, from Brooklyn Heights looking northwest to Manhattan, with the two World Trade Towers (center, 1973-2001).

In Region R1: from Zagreb (Croatia) to Bujumbura (Burundi)

- The sub-region R10 will have the capitals in Zagreb (Croatia) and Brazzaville (Congo) - assistance from Nantes (France).
- The sub-region R11 will have the capitals in Vienna (Austria), Windhoek (Namibia) - assistance from Bilbao (Spain).
- The sub-region R12 will have the capitals in Stockholm (Sweden), Bangui (Central African Republic) - assistance from Florence (Italy).
- The sub-region R13 will have the capitals in Budapest (Hungary), Rundu (Namibia) - assistance from Monaco (Monaco).
- The sub-region R14 will have the capitals in Belgrade (Serbia), Kananga (Democratic Republic of Congo) - assistance from Liverpool (UK).
- The sub-region R15 will have the capitals in Athens (Greece), Mongu (Zambia) - assistance from Los Angeles (CA, USA).
- The sub-region R16 will have the capitals in Helsinki (Finland) and Kolwezi (Democratic Republic of the Congo) - assistance from Montreal (Canada).
- The sub-region R17 will have the capitals in Bucharest (Romania) and Gaborone (Botswana) - assistance from Philadelphia (PA, USA).
- The sub-region R18 will have the capitals in Minsk (Belarus) and Maseru (Lesotho) - assistance from Orleans (France).
- The sub-region R19 will have the capitals in Chisinau (Republic of Moldova) and Bujumbura (Burundi) - assistance from Hamburg (Germany).

USA: New York, the southwest side of the Chase Bank building
(1957-1961, 60 floors (plus 5 below ground), 248 m height, 213,675
m^2, 37 elevators) on Liberty Street, seen here from Pine Street
looking north (Nassau St after the building, William St to the right),
president then David Rockefeller (1915 (age 101 in 2016), studied
at Harvard (1936 cum laude), London School of Economics, and
University of Chicago (1940, Ph. D. in economics), worth $3.1 B).

In Region R2: from Kiev (Ukraine) to Baghdad (Iraq)

- The sub-region R20 will have the capitals in Kiev (Ukraine) and Kigali (Rwanda) - assistance from Ottawa (Canada).
- The sub-region R21 will have the capitals in Ankara (Turkey) and Khartoum (Sudan) - assistance from Salzburg (Austria).
- The sub-region R22 will have the capitals in Lilongwe (Malawi) and Nicosia (Cyprus) - assistance from Dallas (TX, USA).
- The sub-region R23 will have the capitals in Jerusalem (Israel) and Dodoma (Tanzania) - assistance from Strasbourg (France).
- The sub-region R24 will have the capitals in Damascus (Syria) and Nairobi (Kenya) - assistance from Stuttgart (Germany).
- The sub-region R25 will have the capitals in Krasnodar (Russia) and Addis Ababa (Ethiopia) - assistance from Marseille (France).
- The sub-region R26 will have the capitals in Rostov-on-Don (Russia) and Asmara (Eritrea) - assistance from Leipzig (Germany).
- The sub-region R27 will have the capitals in Stavropol (Russia) and Djibouti (Djibouti) - assistance from Zürich (Switzerland).
- The sub-region R28 will have the capitals in Mosul (Iraq) and Moroni (Comoros) - assistance from Linz (Austria).
- The sub-region R29 will have the capitals in Yerevan (Armenia) and Baghdad (Iraq) - assistance from Göttingen (Germany).

Japan: Osaka, ladies in kimono (means thing to wear, now it is very formal and polite clothing, generally worn with traditional footwear (zori or geta) and with split-toe socks (tabi)).

UK, London: The northwest façade of the Old Vic Theatre (1818, 1871, 1902, 1950, 1960, 1963, 1985, 2003, 1067 capacity), on the corner of The Cut and Waterloo Rd., a traditional playhouse with big name actors (Laurence Olivier (1907-1989)) and top directors.

In Region R3: from Riyadh (Saudi Arabia) to Malé (Maldives)

- The sub-region R30 will have the capitals in Riyadh (Saudi Arabia) and Mogadishu (Somalia) - assistance from Bonn (Germany).
- The sub-region R31 will have the capitals in Baku (Azerbaijan) and Antananarivo (Madagascar) - assistance from Le Mans (France).
- The sub-region R32 will have the capitals in Oral (Kazakhstan) and Tehran (Iran) - assistance from Pisa (Italy).
- The sub-region R33 will have the capitals in Ashgabat (Turkmenistan) and Abu Dhabi (United Arab Emirates) - assistance from Wolfsburg (Germany).
- The sub-region R34 will have the capitals in Magnitogorsk (Russia) and Muscat (Oman) - assistance from Toulouse (France).
- The sub-region R35 will have the capitals in Chelyabinsk (Russia) and Herat (Afghanistan) - assistance from Basel (Switzerland).
- The sub-region R36 will have the capitals in Tyumen (Russia) and Kandahar (Afghanistan) - assistance from Nagoya (Japan).
- The sub-region R37 will have the capitals in Dushanbe (Tajikistan) and Labytnangi (Russia) - assistance from Limoges (France).
- The sub-region R38 will have the capitals in Tashkent (Uzbekistan) and Kabul (Afghanistan) - assistance from Rostock (Germany).
- The sub-region R39 will have the capitals in Islamabad (Pakistan) and Malé (Maldives) - assistance from La Rochelle (France).

Japan: Looking to Hotel Keihan Temmashi Osaka (2nd from right, operated by Keihan Electric Railway, 800 m northwest of Osaka Castle and 300 m south of the river)), Osaka Merchandise store (center right big), the beginning of the bridge over the river (center).

UK, London: From Newington Butts, in front of the west entrance to the Elephant and Castle Shopping Centre, a small statue Elephant and Castle, and a tall building (left back) with 3 holes on top.

In Region R4: from Bishkek (Kyrgyzstan) to Brahmapur (India)

- The sub-region R40 will have the capitals in Bishkek (Kyrgyzstan) and Jaipur (India) - assistance from Osaka (Japan).
- The sub-region R41 will have the capitals in Akola (India) and Kashgar (China) - assistance from Genoa (Italy).
- The sub-region R42 will have the capitals in Almaty (Kazakhstan) and Coimbatore (India) - assistance from Perth (Australia).
- The sub-region R43 will have the capitals in Kuybyshev (Russia) and Agra (India) - assistance from Fukuoka (Japan).
- The sub-region R44 will have the capitals in Vertikos (Russia) and Nagpur (India) - assistance from Coral Bay (Australia).
- The sub-region R45 will have the capitals in Chennai (India) and Colombo (Sri Lanka) - assistance from Sapporo (Japan).
- The sub-region R46 will have the capitals in Lucknow (India) and Fedosikha (Russia) - assistance from Niigata (Japan).
- The sub-region R47 will have the capitals in Bilaspur (India) and Kolpashevo (Russia) - assistance from Albany (Australia).
- The sub-region R48 will have the capitals in Visakhapatnam (India) and Barnaul (Russia) - assistance from Hiroshima (Japan).
- The sub-region R49 will have the capitals in Brahmapur (India) and Tomsk (Russia) - assistance from Yokohama (Japan).

Australia: Sydney Monorail (1988, closed after 25 years in 2013, 3.6 km, connected Darling Harbour (in photo), Chinatown and the Sydney central business and shopping districts, 8 stations, 6 trains).

Japan: Osaka, a copy of the Statue of Liberty (right up), ads for Camel (up right yellow), AIU Insurance Company (center right white), route 3 for Kobe left after 800 m.

In Region R5: from Kathmandu (Nepal) to Dehong (China)

- The sub-region R50 will have the capitals in Kathmandu (Nepal) and Patna (India) - assistance from Kobe (Japan).

- The sub-region R51 will have the capitals in Bayingol (China) and Novokuznetsk (Russia) - assistance from Vichy (France).

- The sub-region R52 will have the capitals in Thimphu (Bhutan) and Dhaka (Bangladesh) - assistance from Jena (Germany).

- The sub-region R53 will have the capitals in Lhasa (China) and Achinsk (Russia) - assistance from Reims (France).

- The sub-region R54 will have the capitals in Abakan (Russia) and Kumul (China) - assistance from Fribourg (Switzerland).

- The sub-region R55 will have the capitals in Kyzyl (Russia) and Dibrugarh (India) - assistance from Denmark (Australia).

- The sub-region R56 will have the capitals in Bassein (Myanmar) and Tinsukia (India) - assistance from Chiba (Japan).

- The sub-region R57 will have the capitals in Yushu City (China) and Tinskoy (Russia) - assistance from Klagenfurt (Austria).

- The sub-region R58 will have the capitals in Jiuquan (China) and Medan (Indonesia) - assistance from Lucerne (Switzerland).

- The sub-region R59 will have the capitals in Chiang Mai (Thailand) and Dehong (China) - assistance from Mulhouse (France).

Australia: Near Sydney Opera House, looking south to business and residential tall buildings.

Japan: On a freeway near Osaka, with an ad for National Panasonic (right), Osaka Airport left after 800 m.

In Region R6: from Bangkok (Thailand) to Chita (Russia)

- The sub-region R60 will have the capitals in Bangkok (Thailand) and Kuala Lumpur (Malaysia) - assistance from Besançon (France).
- The sub-region R61 will have the capitals in Vientiane (Laos) and Singapore – assistance from Freiburg im Breisgau (Germany).
- The sub-region R62 will have the capitals in Phnom Penh (Cambodia) and Irkutsk (Russia) – assistance from Baden (Switzerland).
- The sub-region R63 will have the capitals in Palembang (Indonesia), Hanoi (Vietnam) – assistance from Thun (Switzerland).
- The sub-region R64 will have the capitals in Ulan Bator (Mongolia) and Ulan-Ude (Russia) – assistance from Chaumont (France).
- The sub-region R65 will have the capitals in Cirebon (Indonesia) and Nanning (China) – assistance from Vaduz (Lichtenstein).
- The sub-region R66 will have the capitals in Pontianak (Indonesia) and Baotou (China) – assistance from Lugano (Switzerland).
- The sub-region R67 will have the capitals in Surakarta (Indonesia) and Yichang (China) – assistance from Thonon-les-Bain (France).
- The sub-region R68 will have the capitals in Surabaya (Indonesia) and Changsha (China) – assistance from Burgdorf (Switzerland).
- The sub-region R69 will have the capitals in Chita (Russia) and Hong Kong (China) – assistance from Colmar (France).

UK, London: At the east end of Westminster Bridge (1862, 250 m, width 26 m, 7 spans, right) over Thames (flowing left to right), Palace of Westminster (1016, 1870, 300 m river front façade, 1,100 rooms, center left, with Victoria Tower (1858, 98 m, left), and Central Tower (91 m)), Big Ben (1855, 96 m, center right).

USA: 3 Dec 2009, from Harvard Medical School looking northeast to the Avenue Louis Pasteur (1822-1895, French microbiologist),

In Region R7: from Nanchang (China) to Melbourne (Australia)

- The sub-region R70 will have the capitals in Bandar Seri Begawan (Brunei Darussalam) and Nanchang (China) – assistance from Turku (Finland).
- The sub-region R71 will have the capitals in Krasnokamensk (Russia) and Jinan (China) – assistance from St. Gallen (Switzerland).
- The sub-region R72 will have the capitals in Baguio City (Philippines) and Hangzhou (China) – assistance from Dole (France).
- The sub-region R73 will have the capitals in Manila (Philippines) and Taipei (Taiwan, China) – assistance from Metz (France).
- The sub-region R74 will have the capitals in Kupang (Indonesia) and Shanghai (China) – assistance from Davos (Switzerland).
- The sub-region R75 will have the capitals in Pyongyang (North Korea) and Seoul (South Korea) – assistance from Versailles (France).
- The sub-region R76 will have the capitals in Vladivostok (Russia) and Busan (South Korea) – assistance from Innsbruck (Austria).
- The sub-region R77 will have the capitals in Kyoto (Japan) and Khabarovsk (Russia) – assistance from Germering (Germany).
- The sub-region R78 will have the capitals in Nagoya (Japan) and Komsomolsk-on-Amur (Russia) – assistance from Venice (Italy).
- The sub-region R79 will have the capitals in Sendai (Japan) and Melbourne (Australia) – assistance from St. Moritz (Switzerland).

On a street in Sydney (1788, 5 M people, southeast of Australia), with a sign showing the direction to the Opera House. (1959-1973, 183 m by 120 m by 65 m height, total seating capacity 5738)).

In Region R8: from Anchorage (Alaska, USA) to Lima (Peru)

- The sub-region R80 will have the capitals in Uelen (Russia) and Anchorage (Alaska, USA), – assistance from Zug (Switzerland).
- The sub-region R81 will have the capitals in Vancouver (Canada) and San Jose (CA, USA) – assistance from Odense (Denmark).
- The sub-region R82 will have the capitals in Vernon (Canada) and Los Angeles (CA, USA) – assistance from Amstetten (Austria).
- The sub-region R83 will have the capitals in Calgary (Canada) and Tijuana (Mexico) – assistance from Chur (Switzerland).
- The sub-region R84 will have the capitals in Hermosillo (Mexico) and Tucson (AR, USA) – assistance from Bergen (Norway).
- The sub-region R85 will have the capitals in Chihuahua (Mexico) and Regina (Canada) – assistance from Gothenburg (Sweden).
- The sub-region R86 will have the capitals in San Luis Potosi City (Mexico) and Winnipeg (Canada) – assistance from Yverdon-les-Bains (Switzerland).
- The sub-region R87 will have the capitals in Tulsa (OK, USA) and Veracruz (Mexico) – assistance from Bregenz (Austria).
- The sub-region R88 will have the capitals in Memphis (TN, USA) and San José (Costa Rica) – assistance from Uppsala (Sweden).
- The sub-region R89 will have the capitals in Lima (Peru) and Boston (MA, USA) – assistance from Tampere (Finland).

Japan: Kyoto, at a temple where it is customary to touch a sculpture.

UK, London: From the Bridge Street, at the northwest corner of Big Ben, looking south to the northwest garden (right) and entrances (left and back) of the Palace of Westminster (1016).

In Region R9: from La Paz (Bolivia) to London (United Kingdom)

- The sub-region R90 will have the capitals in La Paz (Bolivia) and Bangor (Maine, USA) – assistance from Aosta (Italy).
- The sub-region R91 will have the capitals in Caracas (Venezuela) and Road Town (British Virgin Islands) – assistance from Obergoms (Switzerland).
- The sub-region R92 will have the capitals in Buenos Aires (Argentina) and Fort-de-France (Martinique) – assistance from Freudenstadt (Germany).
- The sub-region R93 will have the capitals in Asuncion (Paraguay) and Montevideo (Uruguay) – assistance from Winterthur (Switzerland).
- The sub-region R94 will have the capitals in Cayenne (French Guiana), St. John's (Canada) – assistance from Novara (Italy).
- The sub-region R95 will have the capitals in Rio de Janeiro (Brazil) and Dakar (Senegal) – assistance from Toyama (Japan).
- The sub-region R96 will have the capitals in Freetown (Sierra Leone) and Lisbon (Portugal) – assistance from Kawasaki (Japan).
- The sub-region R97 will have the capitals in Bamako (Mali) and Athlone (Ireland) – assistance from Ulm (Germany).
- The sub-region R98 will have the capitals in Yamoussoukro (Cote d'Ivoire) and Madrid (Spain) – assistance from Okayama (Japan).
- The sub-region R99 will have the capitals in Ouagadougou (Burkina Faso) and London (United Kingdom) - assistance from Vaasa (Finland).

Japan: Kyoto, Toji Temple, with a wooden pagoda, and sculptures of deities from around 750, 1 km southwest of Kyoto Tower.

UK, London: From the Broad Sanctuary, west of St. Margaret's Church, looking to the north façade (north entrance (left)) of Westminster Abbey (960, 1517, Collegiate Church of St Peter at Westminster, Anglican abbey hosting daily services, and every coronation since 1066, tower height 69 m, floor area 3,000 m^2).

Question 12. How is the Level 3 Management?

Response 12: The ten L3 friendly managers for the 10 regions are presented in point 5.4:

5.4. Level 3 Management: Ten L3 friendly managers for the 10 regions, who will supervise and assist the 10 L2 managers of the 10 sub-regions of each region, for a total of about 770,000,000 people for each region.

- The Region R0 will have the first capitals in

Bern (Switzerland) and Libreville (Gabon) – assistance from Oxford (UK).

For better quality and consistency of the management, we'll have the first two cities from the region R0, and the third city from outside. Actually, being inside the same country Terra, any city, sub-region or region can ask for advice or help from anybody.

- The Region R1 will have the first capitals in

Warsaw (Poland) and Pretoria (South Africa) – assistance from Miami (FL, USA).

- The Region R2 will have the first capitals in

Moscow (Russia) and Cairo (Egypt) – assistance from Grenoble (France).

- The Region R3 will have the first capitals in

Astana (Kazakhstan) and Karachi (Pakistan), – assistance from Montpellier (France).

Japan: Kyoto, a bust of Ludwig van Beethoven (1770 in Bonn, Germany – 1827 in Vienna, Austria, very famous German composer) on a balcony of a small house.

UK, London: From the Shard (244 m), looking west to (from right down): railroad bridge (Cannon St Station), Southwalk Bridge, Millennium Bridge, another railroad bridge, Blackfriars Bridge, and Waterloo Bridge.

- The Region R4 will have the first capitals in

New Delhi (India) and Novosibirsk (Russia) – assistance from Magdeburg (Germany).

- The Region R5 will have the first capitals in

Krasnoyarsk (Russia) and Urumqi (China) – assistance from Avignon (France).

- The Region R6 will have the first capitals in

Jakarta (Indonesia) and Beijing (China) – assistance from Neuchâtel (Switzerland).

- The Region R7 will have the first capitals in

Tokyo (Japan) and Sydney (Australia) – assistance from Malmö (Sweden).

- The Region R8 will have the first capitals in

Washington (USA) and Mexico City (Mexico) – assistance from Bellinzona (Switzerland).

- The Region R9 will have the first capitals in

Halifax (Canada) and Brasilia (Brazil) – assistance from Biel (Switzerland).

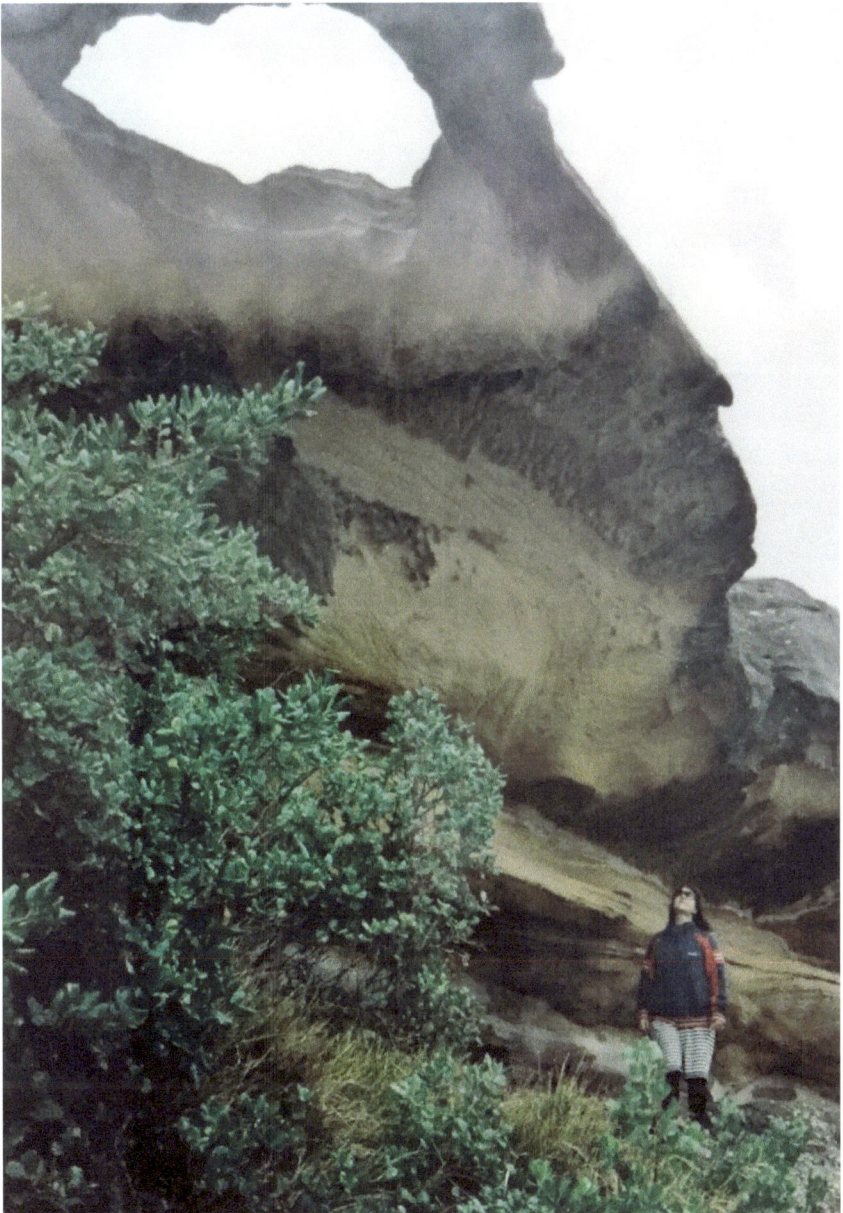

In eastern Australia, in south-eastern Sydney, 20 km south of the Sydney Opera House, 16 km southeast of the Sydney central business district, on the west shore of the Pacific Ocean, 80 m northeast of the Bare Island (discovered by James Cook in 1770), 200 m southwest of the Congwong Beach, 200 m southeast of Lapérouse Museum, looking up to a rock with a hole in the center.

Question 13. What about the Level 4 Management?

Response 13: The level 4 Management are the very friendly 10 Advisers of the world, as described in point 5.5:

5.5. Level 4 Management: very friendly 10 Advisers

5.5.1 - L4 very friendly 10 Advisers of the world, who will supervise and assist the 10 L3 managers of the 10 regions of the Earth, for a total of about 7,700,000,000 people – all the people on Earth, citizens of Peaceful Terra.

Sweden, Malmö, from Skeppsbron looking north to the north part of the west side of the Central Station (right), sign for Trelleborg and Limhamn (to left), Goteborg and Hamnen (straight).

Question 14. Where will the 10 Advisors be located?

Response 14: They will be located each in one the ten Regions R0, R1,…, R9, as explained in the following points:

5.5.2 - The L4 very friendly 10 Advisers of the world will be located each in one the ten Regions R0, R1,…, R9. For example, in the beginning, for the first month (then changing every month), the ten Advisers of the world will be located:

- in R0: Barcelona (Spain)
- in R1: Benghazi (Libya)
- in R2: Addis Ababa (Ethiopia)
- in R3: Hyderabad (Pakistan)
- in R4: Bhopal (India)
- in R5: Mandalay (Myanmar)
- in R6: Nanchong (China)
- in R7: Khabarovsk (Russia)
- in R8: Houston (USA)
- in R9: Recife (Brazil)

5.5.3 – These ten L4 Advisers will be in permanent contact with each other, and with the L3 Advisers, for the best management of the world.

5.5.7 – The ten L4 Advisers will move each month from a first capital of a region to the second capital of another region, at random (or based on urgency, if an emergency occurred). This mobility is essential for having a long period of tranquility and harmony.

5.5.22 - The Advisors will be located in the current government buildings, and the excess government buildings and properties will be sold, in order to increase the budget, and to reduce the expenses.

5.5.26 - The top 10 Advisers (and all the others) will collaborate via e-mail, telephone, videoconferences, mail, or face to face, when needed, to produce practical results for all people, very fast.

UK, London: St James's Park (23 ha) Lake, looking west to the east façade of the Buckingham Palace (600 m away, 1703, 1850, 1913, 24 m height).

Question 15. How will the 10 Advisors take decisions?

Response 15: By consensus only, as per point 5.5.4:

5.5.4 – The ten L4 Advisers will work by consensus only.

It is expected that the 10 Advisors are talented enough to be able to negotiate fast any disagreements between them, and quickly arrive at the best common decision, for the benefit of all people.

Italy, Roma - Arco di Tito (Arch of Titus, 82 AD, restored in 1821, left), and the church Santa Francesca Romana (975 – 1615, right).

Question 16. How will the 10 Advisors be elected?

Response 16: They will be elected from the 10 regions, as per points 5.5.5 and 5.5.6:

5.5.5 - The ten L4 Advisers will be elected from the 10 regions, and each of them will be the First Adviser (*First among equals* – from Latin: Primus inter pares) for one month, by rotation.

5.5.6 - The First Adviser only coordinates the work of the other 9 Advisors for one month.

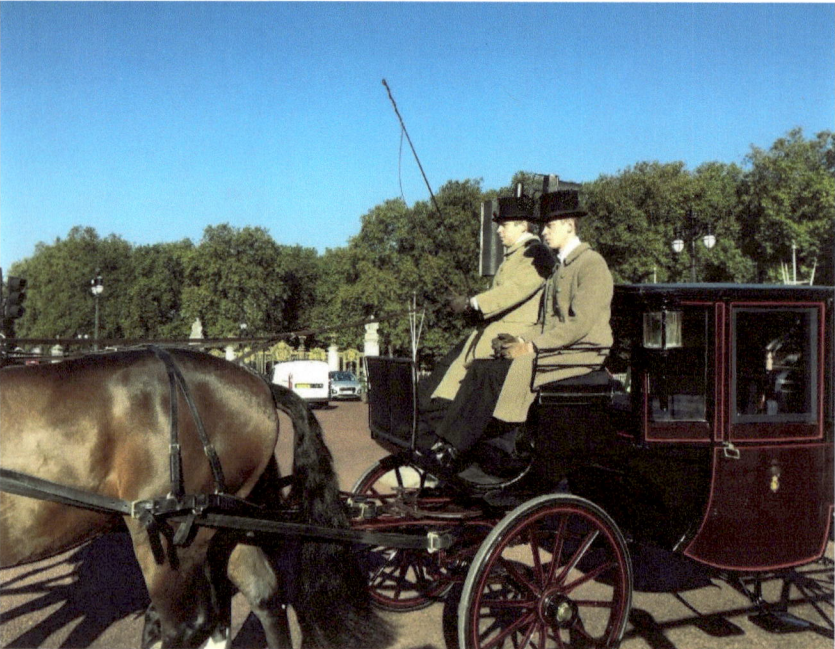

UK, London: Near the Buckingham Palace (1703, 1850, 1913), a traditional horse (Cleveland Bay) drawn carriage (Clarence (Brougham), 1810 style).

Question 17. How will the 10 Advisors inform the people?

Response 17: By using a Monthly World Report, as per following points:

5.5.8 - The First Adviser, on the last day of each month, will present in writing for the world (no more than 5 standard pages) a clear and precise Monthly World Report, with a list of finished and unfinished tasks.

5.5.9 - The other 9 Advisers will add their comments to the Monthly World Report (no more than half a page each - total report less than 9.5 pages).

5.5.23 - In order to better know the world government, to help it, and, especially, to improve it, all able people of the world will work as volunteers at least one day per year in each of the seven departments.

5.5.24 - After each Monthly World Report, a public opinion survey about the report should be taken, and presented to all Advisors.

5.5.25 - All activities of the Advisors, and others from the small World Government, will be available to the people on a website.

London - The program by Candlelight at St Martin in the Fields, on Friday, Oct. 14, 2016 at 7:30 PM, with Antonio Vivaldi (1678 in Venice-1741 (age 63) Vienna), Johann Sebastian Bach (1685-1750 (age 65)), Francesco Geminiani (1687-1762 (age 75)), George Frideric Handel (1685 Germany-1759 (age 74) London), Wolfgang Amadeus Mozart (1756 Salzburg-1791 (age 35) Vienna), Johann Pachelbel (1653 Nuremberg-1706 (age 53) Nuremberg, Germany).

Question 18. What are Advisors' management responsibilities?

Response 18: They manage all Government Departments, as per 5.5.10 – 5.5.17 and 5.5.21:

5.5.10 - The top 10 Advisers will manage Police and all other Departments.

5.5.11 - For obvious uncooperative or improper attitude of one top Advisor X, the other 9 can replace X with X's number 2, and X will receive appropriate medical treatment.

5.5.12 - When vacancies happen for Advisors, the number 2 for those Advisors will fill the vacancies.

5.5.13 - All the activities of all Advisors will be recorded in computers and videos, and on paper, for people to be able to see what they are doing.

5.5.14 - Advisors at all levels should work 40 hours/week, with 4 weeks of vacation, but many services (medical, police (firemen should be part of the police), emergency, volunteers) should be non-stop.

5.5.15 – Advisors' compensation should be the world annual average salary (in 2019 less than $10,000) plus 4% of that world average salary, for level 4 (total $10,400), + 3 % for level 3, and so on. They all should work to increase the world average salary, in order to get themselves an increase.

5.5.16 - All the other world government employees will have a compensation close to the average compensation of the people in the area where they are located.

5.5.17 - All Advisors are free to speak about their administrative work, with modesty.

5.5.21 - At least 7 of the top 10 Advisers should be present every working day.

UK, London: The southwest façade (center left) and the southeast side (center right) of the St Peter's Church (1827, Eaton Square, Belgravia).

Question 19. Who can declare war?

Response 19: Nobody! It is very clear from points 5.5.19 and 5.5.20:

5.5.19 - Advisors (and all the others) cannot declare war, reprisals or capture land or water.

5.5.20 - Advisors (and all the others) cannot raise and support armies, navy, or any military forces.

UK, London: From a boat on Thames (flowing left to right), looking west to the east façade of The Royal Horseguards hotel (1884 building inspired from Château de Chambord (1547, Vallée de la Loire, Architect Domenico da Cortona), with Whitehall Gardens (from Palace of Whitehall (1240-1698) in front and Victoria Embankment (by river)

Question 20. Who will help the management?

Response 20: Each Advisor, and each manager at all levels, will have 5 immediate assistants, as described in the following points:

5.6.1 - Each Advisor, and each manager at all levels, will have 5 immediate assistants:
1) a mathematician for finance and all other calculations,
2) a medical doctor for keeping everybody healthy, calm, polite, friendly and optimist,
3) a CEO for good management,
4) an engineer for all practical projects, and
5) a teacher for education, training and related areas.

5.6.2 – The five assistants play a key role, because they are highly qualified professionals, who actually will carry on the practical management of the world.

5.6.3 - The five assistants' integrity, professionalism and friendliness will significantly improve the quality of the world and local governments.

5.6.4 - The five assistants are really the experts. They will assist the Advisors and all levels of management, in order to have an efficient, correct and professional working of the world government at all levels.

5.5.18 - All spending proposals from Advisers must be approved by their 5 assistants (doctors, mathematicians, CEOs, engineers and teachers), and must have an already existing funding in the budget.

Italy, Udine: 3 Nov 2009, Piazza San Giacomo (200 m west of Piazza della Liberta, and 300 m southwest of Castello di Udine), named before Piazza di Mercatonuovo or delle Erbe, now also called Piazza Matteotti, with Chiesa San Giacomo (1378, façade 1525, Cappella delle Anime (above the clock) 1744), and a column (1487) with the Virgin statue.

Question 21. Who will oversee the top management?

Response 21: An Honorific World Observer, as presented in the following points:

5.7.1 - A Honorific World Observer will be quietly elected by direct vote – starting, for example, 1st September 2022 - for only one 3 years term, with the main duty to observe that the top 10 Advisers efficiently perform their duties, and keep their words – if they don't, they will be changed.

5.7.2 - For managers and for everybody else, keeping their word is a serious and strict requirement.

5.7.3 - The Honorific World Observer has this responsibility for the top 10 Advisors, but all people will pay attention to this. Words must become again important and respected.

Question 22. How the World Government looks like?

Response 22: The World Government will have only 7 Departments, and there are some other important details:

5.8.1 - All the employees of the World Government are temporary, and must reapply for their positions every year.

5.8.2 – There is no need for unions.

5.8.3 - The World Government will be limited to:
1) the Office of the Honorific Observer (less than 10 employees),
2) the Office of the top ten Advisors (less than 100 employees), and
3) 7 small departments.

Australia: A big and old tree in the Royal Botanic Gardens, south of the Sydney Opera House, with the Sydney Harbour (center left).

Question 23. Which are the 7 World Government Departments?

Response 23: They are presented in 5.8.4:

5.8.4 - The World Government will have these 7 small departments:

- Tax Department

- Collects taxes of 15% of the income of people and revenue of companies.

- The Manager of the Tax Department is appointed for a three-year term by the World 10 Advisers.

- The number of employees must be under 50,000, with excellent computers, and advanced software.

Switzerland, Geneva, from Quai Gustave Ador (1845-1928, President). Jet d'Eau (1886, 1891, 1951) – a large fountain pumping lake water at 500 liters/s to 140 m, lit up at night. It is located at the point where Lac Léman empties into the Rhône River. There are two 500 kW pumps, operating at 2,400 V, consuming one megawatt of electricity. The water leaves the nozzle (10.16 cm) at a speed of 200 km/h. At any time, there are about 7,000 liters of water in the air.

- Treasury

Treasury will control all the financial issues, including:
- antitrust
- fiscal service
- financial cooperation
- financing bank
- world reserve system
- world budget using only revenue, no borrowing, and spending only on strict necessary needs
– all the budgets, at all levels, will have a 2% surplus, which will be returned to the taxpayers
- register of all government papers and activities
- archives and records
- assist all people to have savings accounts for old age (the old age will be starting around 70), and 10% of their income should automatically go to their savings accounts. For those unable to work, their doctors and mathematicians will decide case by case.
- bankruptcies, in general, will be discouraged, and when strict necessary, will be analyzed and solved, case by case, by the doctors, mathematicians and CEOs who worked with the people who asked the bankruptcy.
- encourage all families to assist their parents, grandparents, and great-grandparents.
- housing finance
- housing for all people
- no homelessness
- consumer financial protection
- pensions
- privacy
- current social security until replaced by personal savings
- personnel management
- general services for the world government
- each the 10 regions will receive 2.5% of the world taxes - at least 30% of the money will be sent to villages and cities.
- each of the 100 sub-regions will receive 0.25% of the world taxes. At least 40% of the money will be sent to villages and cities.

- The World Central Bank will include all current central banks – starting, for example, on May 1st, 2023.
- The Special Credit Card (SCC) will be issued by the World Central Bank.
- Advisors will create a new world currency, named, for example, "coin", and all the other currencies will be exchanged for coins. The World Central Bank will implement the details.
- The counterfeiting and all other bad things, which some sick people do, will be medically treated (in specialized medical institutions when necessary), and those who did bad things will pay all the expenses, and will reimburse the victims. Victims will always be very protected, and helped to recover the losses from the attackers.

3 Nov 2009, from Piazzale del Castello, looking east to the northwest side of Castello di Udine (983, 1517-1567, 138 m).

- People Assistance Department

It will assist people in general, including:
- parent assistance
- dispute resolution
- in very simple disputes or culpa levis (ordinary negligence, like late payments, etc.), one single assistant will decide within minutes, and all people will go back to work
- census every 5 years
- election assistance every 20 months
 - special credit cards
- people protection against abuses from anybody
- completely eliminate corruption, organized crime and drug trafficking
- all people in the world will remain in their places, and the improvements will come to them. Those who want to move to other places, will need first a special invitation from at least 10 people (not family related) where they want to move.
- all the Tribunals and related areas will be transformed in people assistance services, based on friendliness, collaboration and goodwill.
- It is well understood that no excessive bail will be required, no excessive fines imposed, no cruel and unusual punishments applied, but, at the same time, it is well understood that a person who did a bad thing will receive the necessary corrective medical treatment, and will reimburse all people who suffered damages, and the medical treatment. The victims will always receive special attention.
- Nobility (King, Prince, etc.) could continue to exist in some places, but they should not interfere with activities of the Advisors, and actually should help them.
- food safety
- trash & recycling
- free commerce
- jobs assistance
- postal service
- labor safety and harmonious relations
- land, water

- volunteers
- fitness, sport, tourism
- 10 world holidays: the normal 4 Earth events (2 solstices (around 21 June, around 21 December), and 2 equinoxes (around 21 March, around 21 September), Mother's Day on 1st May, Father's Day on 6 August, Children's Day on 6 November, Grandparents' Day on 6 February, and 2 optional days (like Thanksgiving or a Religious Day (Christmas), and New Year).

Italy, Venezia - Procuratie Nuove (right), Fermata San Marco (center-right), Giardini Reali (right), Chiesa San Fantin (in the back, near Teatro La Fenice), Capitano di Porto (center), Palazzo Giustinian (center-left), at the east entrance in the Canal Grande.

- Medical Department

It will manage all medical and healthcare related areas, including:
- human services
- conflict resolution
- families, children, elderly
- medicine approval
- disease control and prevention
- medical doctors and assistants will make regular home visits, at least once a year, to all people, to keep them healthy, and to prevent illnesses.
- medical research: cancer, heart, lung, blood, arthritis, surgical robotics, connected computers for healthcare, etc.
- healthy homes, streets, stores, working places, etc.
- healthy aging
- all misunderstandings, disagreements or conflicts of any nature will be treated by medical personnel (with police help when strict necessary), until all is back to normal.
- no prisons are necessary, only specialized medical institutions (in simple cases, the places where the treated people live can be used, with the necessary limitations and surveillance)
- If a person X is considered that did a bad thing, X will have, within 3 days, a discussion with one or more doctors and other assistants, and will be informed of the nature and cause of the bad thing; including witnesses against and for him. Then a decision will be taken within other 3 days, by a group of doctors and other assistants. Victims of bad people will always have priority to discuss their problems with one or more doctors and other assistants, and quick decisions will be taken within 3 days, by a group of doctors and other assistants. Protection of victims has always priority.
- in order to better know the world government, to help it, and, especially, to improve it, all able people of the world will work as volunteers at least one day per year in the local facility of this department, which will have a special office for managing this volunteer work.

– all people will have government medical insurance, and they can also have private medical insurance

– there will be doctors working for the government 100%, or only part-time, or having only private practice, all with reasonable salaries and fees.

– there will be government pharmaceutical institutions and private pharmaceutical companies, offering reasonable priced medicines, without advertising to the general public.

UK, London, from Parliament Square, looking southwest to the Church of St Margaret of Antioch (1523, the Anglican parish church of the House of Commons), 20 m northeast of the Westminster Abbey.

Italy, Venezia - The Clock Tower (Torre dell'Orologio), 1499. At the top there are two bronze figures, which strike the hours on a bell. The bell was casted at the Arsenal in 1497. Below is the winged lion of Venice. There was a statue of the Doge Agostino Barbarigo (Doge 1486-1501) before the lion. Below the statues of the Virgin and Child. On either side are two large blue panels showing the time: 5:55 PM, the same on the clock below: XVII very close to XVIII.

- Police

Police will provide assistance for:
- accidents
- disasters
- complete elimination of nuclear, chemical and biological arms, firearms and explosives
- world complete security
- world cooperation
- conflict reduction and resolution
- investigations
- emergency assistance
- training
- delinquency prevention in general, and especially juvenile
- protection of Advisors, important government buildings, etc.
- extended surveillance and reconnaissance to prevent bad events
- fire protection
- volunteers to help police
- police will be present at public meetings, services, shows, etc., in order to protect the public
- public order
- ensuring traffic safety
- completely eliminate corruption, organized crime and drug trafficking
- movement of people based on civilized rules
- assist and protect those who have encountered violence
- World Police and specialists from the former United Nations and Interpol will be ready and very mobile for urgent and special operations, when they are needed.
- Police will be the only department which will have some small arms, in order to stop some very bad people (who are very sick).
- a small manufacturing and maintenance of arms unit will be part of the Police Department, under strict control.
- Police will work with medical personnel, mathematicians, CEOs, engineers, teachers and others, to make sure that all the people on the Planet are in good mental health, in order to prevent bad situations. This is also a major responsibility of all Advisors.

- prevention of bad events
- The Advisors will allocate the necessary budget for Police, and Police will assist people in need.

Paris - The central part of the façade of L'Opéra de Paris (1875): composers Daniel Auber (1782–1871, left), Ludwig van Beethoven (1770–1827, second), Wolfgang Amadeus Mozart (1756–1791, center) and Gaspare Spontini (1774–1851, right).

- Education Department

- Over 2 billions of children in the world will get a solid peace-oriented education, to give a solid peace-oriented foundation for a good, free, peaceful and prosperous life.
- Education is very important – teachers will work with parents and grandparents, to educate the children to leave healthy in a sustainable peace, liberty and prosperity.
- Discipline must be strict, and those who do not behave properly, will get medical assistance.
- The world will have 4 school levels (SLs) of education:

SL1 – Kindergarten – 2 years: age 5 and 6

SL2 – Primary School – 4 years: age 7, 8, 9 and 10

SL3 – Secondary School – 3 years: age 11, 12 and 13

SL4 – High School or Vocational School – 4 years: age 14, 15, 16 and 17

- A World Library will include the Library of Congress and all the other great libraries – they will remain where they are now, but will be digitally interconnected, and accessible from any place in the world.
- adult education: technical, career
- training for employment
- management training
- post high school education
- peace education
- world constitution education

3 Nov 2009, Piazza della Liberta, looking east to Porticato di San Giovanni (1533, left), Via Vittorio Veneto (center right back), il Campanile della Chiesa del Duomo (center right up), the column (1539) with San Marco's lion (the symbol of Venezia, right).

- Science & Technology Department.

It will help in the areas of:
- mathematics
- statistics
- science
- technology
- Algorithmic Governance will be an essential tool for a better and impartial governing of the world, used by the Advisers elected by people. Mathematicians from all countries will work to improve the Algorithmic Governance, to better serve the people.
- cyberspace complete security will be achieved and strictly maintained
- information systems
- computer services
- Internet
- scientific cooperation
- economic development at the world level
- infrastructure improvement and maintenance at the world level
- innovation and improvements in all areas, at the world level
- transportation at the world level
- safety
- security
- aviation
- highway
- cars
- railroads without noise
- maritime administration
- logistics
- strategic planning at the world level
- public works
- fleet maintenance
- standards: weights, measures, etc.
- research at the world level
- risk analysis
- laboratories
- engineering

- communications at the world level
- telecommunications
- networks
- peaceful nuclear energy use at the world level
- safety
- waste
- electrical power
- oceanic analysis at the world level
- atmospheric analysis at the global level
- meteorological service and prognosis at the global level
- world resources analysis
- sustainable use of world resources
- geographical and geological activity
- product safety at the global level
- hazardous material and chemical safety
- government broadcasting (radio, tv, Internet, newspaper, etc.) including news, scientific and technical information
- private broadcasting will continue, but the world government must be able to directly inform the people, without intermediaries
- space exploration and expansion at the world level – very important for the future
- patent and trademark
- intellectual rights
- all government work, which can be done by private companies, will be contracted with the best and reasonably priced private companies. At the same time, the government should always have competitive services for people – from plumbing and electrical help, to mortgage and buying or selling a house.

UK, London: On Thames, Leadenhall Building (up center left, 2010, 225 m), 30 St Mary Axe (2004, 180 m, 41 floors, The Gherkin, center, con), Sky Garden bld (up left, 2014, 155 m, 35 floors).

Italy, Venezia - Libreria Sansoviniana (left), Il Campanile (center-left), Palazzo Ducale (right), and a Japanese couple wedding picture.

Question 24. What is the frequency of elections?

Response 24: Every 20 months:

Proposition 6. Elections every 20 months

6.1. The Advisers should be elected every 20 months for one term only. If an Adviser X was elected for a term T1, then the next term T2 will have another Advisor Y. For the next term T3, X can be elected again, but the next term T4 will have a new Adviser, and so on. All levels of Advisers (minimum age 25 years) can be elected, not consecutively, at most 4 times (maximum 80 months = 6 years and 8 months).

6.2 All the employees in Government will respect Seneca's (circa 1,960 years ago) aphorism "To govern is to serve, not to rule", and Hippocrates' (over 2,400 years ago) aphorism "Make a habit of two things: to help; or at least to do no harm."

6.3 Advisers should have exceptional results obtained from their work, and based on these results, plus modesty, moderation, good character, friendliness, sharp mind, wisdom, good morals, and intense desire to help people, they will be elected, without any campaigning, publicity, fundraising, donations, debates, propaganda, political parties, advertising, or similar activities.

6.4 There will be use of advanced digital technology, which opens up entirely new opportunities for developing direct elections, and public control of the institutions, improving the transparency of the election procedure, and taking into account the interests and opinions of each voter (over the age of 21, who are not in a special medical institution for bad behavior or for mental health).

Italy, Roma - Trajan's column was erected in 113 AD in honor of Emperor Trajan. It is located at the Forum of Trajan. The column commemorates Trajan's victories in Dacia (now Romania), and is 42 meters tall, including its base.

Question 25. Is there a serious checking of qualifications?

Response 25: Yes, there is an Election Commission:

6.5. An Election Commission of 110 representatives from the 10 regions and from the 100 sub-regions, elected separately for 5 years, will have to examine the qualifications of all the candidates for Advisers, and for other senior management positions. Unqualified candidates will be asked to improve their qualifications, and then to try again later.

6.6. It is important to refresh the management, and to bring new people to help the big family of 7.7 B people. The older generations, who performed well, will be retained in important roles, because experience and maturity count very much. At least two months before the retirement, they will kindly be asked to transfer their expertise to the younger generation. Even after retirement, they will occasionally be invited to share their expertise.

6.7. In every election, with every winner, will be other two for number 2 and number 3. The number 2 and number 3 for each management position will be used when number 1 is not available (vacation, sick, etc.). They will constantly work for number 1, helping to solve urgent problems for the people.

6.8. Good elections are essential for the future.
There has been a tendency to make elections conflict generating events, with lots of propaganda, false information, heavy donations, unpolite confrontations, bully fundraising, hostile political parties and organizations, unlimited power ambitions, etc.
This will be completely changed into clean, friendly elections, in which people choose between leaders with outstanding results, plus talent to lead people to peace and freedom, modesty, moderation, good character, friendliness, sharp mind, wisdom, good

morals, and intense desire to help people – no campaigning, no publicity, no fundraising, no donations, no debates, no propaganda, no political parties, no advertising, or similar activities.

6.9. All Advisors should also be local Administrators – they must show that they are good managers, and produce practical results for all people.

Italy, Cividale del Friuli: 3 Nov 2009, the northeast sides of Palazzo Comunale (1350-1550), center right Giulio Caesare (100 BC – 44 BC) statue, Largo Boiani (right), to the left Corso Paolino d'Aquileia (726-802, priest, theologian, poet and scholar, who worked for Charlemagne (742-814, Holy Roman Emperor (800-814, Rome), King of the Lombards (774-814, Pavia), King of the Franks (768-814, Nayon)), and was appointed (787) Patriarch of Aquileia with residence at Cividale.

Question 26. Will the people be consulted?

Response: Of course, referendum every three months:

Proposition 7. World Referendum

7.1 - An electronic world referendum will be organized every three months. The main questions will be:

1. Are you satisfied with the Government?
2. What Government work is good?
3. What Government work is not good?
4: Suggestions for improvement:

7.2 - Within two months after each referendum, the Government will respond to the people. Based on the suggestions received, new pro-people rules will be replacing some old rules.

France, Paris, Tour Eiffel (1889, 324 m, 279 m at the 3rd level, looking north-west): Tour Eiffel shadow (center), Pont d'Iéna over La Seine (left down), Avenue de New York (green, on the north side of La Seine), Jardin du Trocadéro (1878, 1937, with the Fountain of Warsaw (center left)), Palais de Chaillot (center up), Port de Suffren (down left), Port de la Bourdonnais (down right), Ave. d'Eylau (up-left, vertical), Av. Albert de Mun (center right).

Question 27. Will the arms continue to outnumber the books?

Response: No way – there will be no arms at all:

Proposition 8. Complete Disarmament

8.1 - Arms will not exist anymore, and only the police will have some small arms. Those who want arms for hunting or sport, will borrow them from police stations, with proper documents, rules and payments.

8.2 - All military units will become strong civilian organizations, working to improve the quality of life for everybody.

8.3 - For practical reasons, the transition from the current imperfect situation to the much better Sustainable Peace and Prosperity Structure (SPPS) will be very smooth: first - all the countries remain as they are, and they will begin – for example on January 1st, 2021 - to negotiate total and complete disarmament, with the help of the United Nations, for 3 months. Then for 5 months will intensely work to eliminate all the arms – either transform them in peaceful tools, or destroy them. Then a continuous verification and monitoring will be implemented, the make sure that the world finally achieved complete disarmament forever!

Question 28. Is census important?

Response: Certainly, for delimitations, special cards, etc.

Proposition 9. Census every 5 years

A census will take place every 5 years – starting, for example, on October 1st, 2023 - and all people will receive a special credit card (SCC), with their photo and other personal data. The delimitations between regions, and between sub-regions, will be adjusted by the census.

Italy, Cividale del Friuli: 3 Nov 2009, on Corso Paolino d'Aquileia, on the bridge of Iacopo da Bissone (1442, 50 m by 3.6 m, height 22.5 m, rock) over Natisone River (flowing from back to front), 150 m southeast of Palazzo Comunale, looking northeast to il Campanile of Monastero Santa Maria in Valle (650, up left) and Natisone River.

Question 29. Will people have some helping cards?

Response: Definitively!

Proposition 10. Special Credit Card (SCC)

The special credit card (SCC) will be used to buy everything, to identify for voting, for census, for travel, for medical assistance, etc.

The current private credit cards will continue to work as usual.

The changes of the delimitations between regions, and also sub-regions, will be inputted on these cards, and no other work is needed.

UK, Cambridge, From the entrance on Queens' Ln, looking west to Queens' College (1448, by Margaret of Anjou (1430-1482)) Old Court (1448-1451).

Question 30. Who are sacred for people?

Response: People!

Proposition 11. People are something sacred for people

The enemies of the people on Earth are not other people, but viruses, microbes, bad bacteria and hundreds of deadly illnesses – all people on Earth will work together against these real enemies for all of us.

Netherlands, 14 Aug 1977, Amsterdam (1275, population 1.3 M, elevation minus 2 m (2 m under the Atlantic Ocean level)): Zijkanaal G, with a bridge for the street s150, and Havenstraat on the left.

Paris - On the façade de l'Opéra de Paris (1875): a statue and the bust of Franz Joseph Haydn (1732 – 1809), prolific and important Austrian Composer. He signed his musical work in Italian: "di me Giuseppe Haydn" (by me Joseph Haydn). He wrote a great number of concertos, masses, operas, piano trios, solo piano compositions, string quartets, symphonies, baritone trios, and Gott erhalte Franz den Kaiser, which was used in Das Lied der Deutschen – Germany's national anthem.

Question 31. Will non-violence be the rule?

Response: Yes, very clearly:

Proposition 12. Non-violence and medical assistance

12.1 - Non-violence is a strict requirement for all activities on Earth.

12.2 - The first rule for everybody on Earth comes from the Hippocratic Oath: Primum non nocere - first do not harm.

UK, London, from Newington Butts, in front of the west entrance to the Elephant and Castle Shopping Centre, a small statue Elephant and Castle, and a tall building (left back) with 3 horizontal holes on top.

Italy, Naples (Napoli, 1500 BC, one of the oldest continuously inhabited cities in the world. The city was refunded as Neápolis around 550 BC, and became a sine qua non of Magna Graecia), the FVNICOLARE building near downtown. The Funicolare Centrale (Central Funicular) is a funicular railway, which is the main part of the metro system for the city of Naples (1928, 1.2 km).

Question 32. Will the doctors be closer to people?

Response: Categorically! Home visits will be the real joy.

12.3 - Medical doctors and assistants will make regular home visits to all people, to keep them healthy, and to prevent illnesses.

UK, Oxford, a Public Library close to Christ Church College (1546) and Merton College (1264, named after Walter de Merton).

Geneva (121 BC under Romans, 375 m elevation, population 200,000, area 16 km^2, 70 km northwest of Mont Blanc (4810 m), 660 km southwest of Göttingen), on Rue de la Servette (to the right, going southeast, near Rue Jean Robert Chouet ((1642-1731, physician and politician) (the street is to the left, going northeast)), a nice building having down the restaurant Le Portail Chez Rui (yellow), 1.6 km northwest from Jet d'Eau, 1.6 km southwest from Palais des Nations (UN), 1.4 km northwest from the Université de Genève (1559, John Calvin (1509-1564, aged 55)).

Question 33. Will the truth resurface?

Response: No question about it!

Proposition 13. Truth only and collaboration

13.1 - People need only truth in order to create a long term peaceful and harmonious society.

13.2 - If someone lies – medical treatment will follow.

UK, Oxford, University of Oxford, School of Anthropology and Museum Ethnography, Institute of Social and Cultural Anthropology, at 51 - 53 Banbury Road.

France, the upper part of the western façade of Cathédrale Notre Dame de Paris (1163 – 1345, 90 m), on the south-eastern part of the Île de la Cité, which is considered the center of Paris, in the fourth arrondissement. The organ has 7,374 pipes, with about 900 classified as historical. It has 110 real stops, five 56-key manuals and a 32-key pedalboard; it is now fully computerized. The Towers at Notre-Dame contain five church bells. The great bourdon bell, Emmanuel, from 1681, 13 t, is located in the South Tower (right).

Question 34. How important is freedom?

Response: It is fundamental for all people.

Proposition 14. Freedom is required

14.1 - Freedom is a fundamental requirement on Earth.

14.2 - It is well understood that this freedom refers to doing good things in a civilized manner, not for war, violence or similar bad things, which are against the wellbeing of the people.

14.3 - Freedom goes hand in hand with responsibility.

14.4 - People can assemble peacefully only.

USA, July 1980, from New York Harbor looking northeast to the southwest sides of the Statue of Liberty and twin towers (1973-2001, 417 m and 415 m, 3.3 km away).

Question 35. How will the economy be?

Response: Free market economy - not perfect, but it will be improved.

14.5 - For economy it is clear that the free market economy, while not perfect, gives the best results, but all people will have the option to choose between friendly private services, and friendly government services. Independent assistants and monitors will make sure that there are no abuses. Sine qua non requirements for happiness are morality and free market.

Italy, 3 Nov 2009, Piazza della Liberta, looking east to Porticato di San Giovanni (1533, left), Via Vittorio Veneto (center right back), il Campanile della Chiesa del Duomo (center right up), the column (1539) with San Marco's lion (the symbol of Venezia, right).

Question 36. What about the religion?

Response: It will be free, and will help people.

14.6 - The religion should be free, and is expected not to interfere with activities of the Advisors, and actually should help people.

France, Paris: The east side of l'Opéra de Paris (or l'Opéra Garnier, 1875), a 1,979-seat opera house, seen from Rue Halévy and Rue Glück.

Question 37. Can people petition the World Government?

Response: Certainly, and the people can change the government.

14.7 - People of course can petition the small Word Government, and can change it anytime, if it does not perform as expected.

Australia: On the North Cronulla beach (300 m, highly hazardous, being unprotected on the Pacific Ocean) looking south to the Cronulla city.

Question 38. Will finally spending be less than revenue?

Response: Yes, indeed:

Proposition 15. Spending less than revenue

All budgets will have surplus of 2% - there will be a strict application of the Latin aphorism: "Sumptus censum ne superset" (Let not your spending exceed your income).

Italy, 20 April 1978, Milano, in Piazza della Scala (Largo Antonio Ghiringhelli (1906-1979, left), looking northwest to the southeast façade of Teatro alla Scala (3 August 1778, capacity 2,800).

Question 39. Will old and new errors be eliminated?

Response: Without question, it is a burning issue:

Proposition 16. Correcting errors

16.1 - Correcting errors is a permanent duty for everybody - Darwin (circa 140 years ago) said "To kill an error is as good a service as, and sometimes even better than, the establishing of a new truth or fact."

USA, Cambridge, 23 September 2009, on the campus of Harvard University (1636) in Cambridge, The Harry Elkins Widener (1885-1912 (died on Titanic)) Memorial Library (1915, Beaux-Arts architecture, 3.5 M of books).

Question 40. Wherever there is a human being, there is an opportunity for what?

Response: A kindness! We all remember Seneca:

Proposition 17. Kindness is a necessity

Kindness is a requirement for everybody.
Seneca (circa 1,960 years ago) said "Wherever there is a human being, there is an opportunity for a kindness."
This is a fundamental idea which must be constantly applied.

Italy, Rome: Accademia Nazionale dei Lincei (1603) in Villa Farnesina (1510). The author was invited to give a lecture here in 1977.

Italy, Rome (753 BC, one of the oldest continuously occupied cities in Europe, called Roma Aeterna (The Eternal City) and Caput Mundi (Capital of the World)), in Villa Borghese (1630), a monument (1905, by Lucien Pallez, donated by the French Government) to Victor Hugo (1802 – 1885, the greatest French writer (Hernani (1830, inspired opera Ernani (1844) by Giuseppe Verdi (1813-1901)), Notre-Dame de Paris (1831), Le roi s'amuse (1832, inspired opera Rigoletto (1851) by Giuseppe Verdi)), Les Misérables (1862), Les Contemplations, La Légendre des siècles)).

Question 41. Will the Government be fixed in some big buildings?

Response: No way, all levels of government will be highly mobile:

Proposition 18. Government mobility

18.1 - All levels of government will be highly mobile - changing of the capitals for the 10 regions, and for the 100 sub-regions, etc.

18.2 - It is necessary to move the government close to the people, to be able to quickly solve the local problems.

18.3 - Locally the people will decide how to better organize themselves, to be more efficient and harmonious, with the help of the world government when necessary. Like in any big family, there will be differences in organization and management, based on their abilities and objectives, but all must be peaceful and harmonious. Conflicts will be promptly resolved by the medical personnel, police, and other assistants.

Italy, Cividale del Friuli: 3 Nov 2009, on the left bank of the Natisone River (flowing from right to left), at the southeast end of the bridge of Iacopo da Bissone (1442, 50 m by 3.6 m, height 22.5 m, rock), 200 m southeast of Palazzo Comunale, looking to the northeast side of the bridge and the right bank of the river, with il Campanile (up right) of il Duomo di Santa Maria Assunta (1457-1529).

Question 42. What will the World Police role be?

Response: To help people everywhere:

Proposition 19. World Police and Assistance

19.1 - The United Nations will change in 2-3 years (for example, by 2024) into World Police and Assistance Organization (WPAO), to help local police in case of big natural disasters or big accidents, and will report to the top 10 Advisers. They will be located in all capitals, and help the locals. When an emergency appears, they will quickly move to solve the emergency.

19.2 - The police powers will be limited, and they will know and be friend with all the people in their jurisdiction – this is the key element of a civilized and peaceful Earth. If they notice a person with bad intentions, they immediately retain that person and call for a medical assistant (and other assistants, if necessary), to analyze and solve the issue very quickly.

19.3 - Police will be people's friends everywhere, and they will always help people.

19.4 - Prevention of bad events is the main objective of everybody. If a bad event occurs, the police and their assistants will eliminate the consequences, reestablish the normal situation, and determine why the bad event occurred, in order to improve their activity, and prevent such bad events in the future.

19.5 - Private property cannot be taken for public use, without just compensation, decided by at least 5 assistants.

19.6 - A person cannot be deprived by government of life, liberty, or property, without having several doctors and other assistants agree: for life – at least 12; for liberty – at least 6; for property – at least 3.

19.7 - A person cannot deprive another person of life, liberty, or property, which, unfortunately, occurs very frequently in the world, and very much effort and energy will be allocated to prevent such bad events.

19.8 - In order to prevent bad things, the police, doctors and their assistants will be in permanent contact with all the people, by visiting them, phone calls, e-mails, tele-videos, and mail, to keep everybody calm and happy.

Slovenia, Ljubljana: 2 Nov 2009, statue of France Preseren (1800-1849, educated at the University of Vienna, the greatest Slovene poet), at Cyril and Methodius Square, in Ljubljana (80 km northeast of Trieste).

Question 43. Will the World Government be open all the time?

Response: Yes, about 66% of the Government will always be working somewhere on the Earth - if people need help, they can always call the Government:

Proposition 20. Non-stop working

About 66% of the people of the world are working at any moment. Therefore, non-stop working of all world government departments – especially medical, police, emergency, volunteers – will be carefully organized.

London - From The Mall, looking southwest to the Victoria Memorial (1911, center left) and to the Buckingham Palace (1703).

Italy, Venezia - The left door on the west façade of Basilica
Cattedrale Patriarcale di San Marco. Above the door we can see the
Winged Lion, the symbol of St. Mark and of Venice, which holds
the book quoting *"Pax Tibi Marce Evangelista Meus"* (Peace to
you, Mark, my evangelist).

Question 44. What about privacy?

Response: Privacy of negotiations and discussions are necessary:

Proposition 21. Privacy of discussions

21.1 - In order to have serious and constructive discussions and negotiations, they must be private.

21.2 - Privacy and discipline are necessary for good government work.

21.3 - The results will be public and preserved, but not the private discussions.

Italy, Venezia - Palazzo Dandolo on Riva degli Schiavoni, 150 m east of Piazza San Marco.

Question 45. Will the Government be polite?

Response: You bet!

Proposition 22. Polite and harmonious government

22.1 - It is a strict requirement for the top management, and for all others, to be highly civilized, polite, courteous, harmonious and efficient.

22.2 - Who wants to work for the world government must have good manners.

22.3 - Harmony in the world starts from the harmony and good manners of the people in the world government.

Proposition 31. Living in harmony

Because all people on Earth want to live in harmony right now, it will be relatively easy to implement this in one good and civilized country. This may include having small, beautiful and commonly agreed fences around properties, because good fences make good neighbors, and also helps with more privacy.

Italy, Venezia - The south façade of Basilica Cattedrale Patriarcale di San Marco, with three of the five domes visible up right.

Germany - 23 March 1978, Freibourg im Breisgau (1120 by Duke Berthold III of Zähringen (1085-1122), elevation 278 m, the south façade of Freiburger Münster (cathedral, 1200, 116 m, J. S. Bach (1685-1750) performed here).

Question 46. Will the conflicts remain for long?

Response: No, all conflicts must not only be quickly resolved, but they also must be transformed in friendships:

Proposition 23. Transformation in friendship

23.1 - All conflicts must not only be quickly resolved, but they must be transformed in friendships. This is very important for long term stability.

23.2 - The medical personnel and others will work diligently to make sure that disputes are resolved, and then a friendship is developed. Only in this way the situation will become stable.

23.3 - People want peace, freedom, health, friendship and prosperity, therefore conflicts should be quickly resolved, and then the corrective medical treatment will include the transformation of hostility and aggressiveness into harmony and friendship.

Proposition 32. Dispute resolution

32.1 - Dispute resolution is not only Government's obligation, but it will be everybody's duty.

32.2 - There will be professional assistance from medical personnel, police, people assistance specialists, volunteers, religious organizations, and many others, but the bottom line is that everybody must avoid disputes.

32.3 - When there are different opinions, just stay calm, express your opinion, listen to others, and continue calm the discussion until a compromise is reached.

32.4 – There is no need to spend much time and energy – let the people decide, and even if your idea is not temporarily accepted, there are chances that in the future you'll have more people agree with you.

Australia: The best-known Three Sisters sandstone rock formation (center left, on the south edge of Katoomba (1879, 8,000 people, elevation 1017 m, 110 km west of Sydney, 39 km southeast of Lithgow)).

Question 47. How will the people communicate?

Response: Using a common language and alphabet:

Proposition 24. Easy Communication

24.1 - As a single big, over 7.7 B, family on Earth, all people must be able to communicate easily with each other.

24.2 - For this reason, a common language and alphabet on Earth are needed. Because English is a de facto common language now, it will be taken as the basis of the world language, let's call it Mundo, which will be taught in all schools, and used in the world government. All the other languages will continue as secondary languages.

24.3 - The same is true for the Latin alphabet, which will be used everywhere, with other alphabets as secondary.

24.4 - The teachers will have a very significant role in implementing this proposition.

Italy, Venezia - Piazza San Marco with Palazzo Ducale (right), Libreria Sansoviniana (next to Palazzo Ducale), Basilica di San Marco (back), Giardini Reali and Il Campanile (center-right), Procuratie Nuove (center to left), Capitano di Porto (left).

London - The west façade and entrance of Westminster Abbey (960, 1517, Collegiate Church of St Peter at Westminster, Anglican abbey with daily services and coronations since 1066, tower height 69 m).

Question 48. What about the global wealth?

Response: It will be carefully used only for peace, freedom and prosperity for all:

Proposition 25. Global wealth for Peace only

25.1 - The 2018 Global Wealth Report from Credit Suisse shows that the total global wealth has reached $317 trillions (circa $41,000/person), which is encouraging, and all this wealth must be used only for peace.

25.2 - Like in any big family, there are differences, because some work more, some spend less, some move faster, and, especially, some are sick – this is the main reason for differences: not all people can be equally sick, some people are sicker than others. However, all the people and the government will work to help each other.

25.3 - It is a major responsibility of the Government to increase the global wealth, and to train those in need to have better working abilities and opportunities.

Italy, Rome (753 BC, one of the oldest continuously occupied cities in Europe, called Roma Aeterna (The Eternal City) and Caput Mundi (Capital of the World)), in Piazza Quirinale, the northeast side of Fountain of Castor (1818), with Obelisco del Quirinale (or Monte Cavallo, 1786, 29 m, from Mausoleum of Augustus (63 BC-14 AD)), and statues of the Dioscuri (Castor and Pollux, twin sons of Zeus and Leda) from the thermal baths of Constantine (272-337), Opus Phidiai on the left.

Question 49. Will the bureaucracy dominate as always?

Response: No way – the goal is no bureaucracy whatsoever!

Proposition 26. No bureaucracy

26.1 - No bureaucracy – this is required by all people, and every day attention will be given for improvements in this direction.

26.2 - In a well-organized country, with all people working together in harmony, this can be accomplished in several years.

27.2 - Constant attention will be focused on avoiding duplication at all levels of the world government – there must be continuous collaboration between all levels, to prevent duplication, and to eliminate it, if it was found.
A vice is nourished by being concealed (from Latin: Alitur vitium vivitque tegendo

Question 50. Will corruption generate new problems again?

Response: Clearly not!

Proposition 27. No corruption, no duplication

27.1 - Everybody will work really hard to completely eliminate corruption, organized crime and drug trafficking.

Australia: From Manly Beach (10 km northeast of Sydney Opera), looking east to the vast Pacific Ocean (165,250,000 km^2, 46% of the Earth's water, 33% of all surface area, larger than all of the Earth's land, 10,911 m the deepest point in the world at the Mariana Trench).

Question 51. Will people get good interest on their savings?

Response: 5%.

Proposition 28. World reserve system

28.1 - Each government department will have some reserves for special situations (natural disasters, big accidents), and the banks will also have good financial reserves.

28.2 - All people will be encouraged to save some money in banks with 5% interest.

USA: California, from Pacifica State Beach (south of San Francisco), looking west to the Pacific Ocean (165,250,000 km^2).

Question 52. Is there concern regarding integrity and efficiency?

Response: Sure – inspectors will help.

Proposition 29. Integrity and efficiency

29.1 - Inspectors will help the Government with the integrity and efficiency issues – always there are ways to improve the work.

29.2 - Inspectors will give advice regarding integrity and efficiency, and will take corrective actions when necessary.

Paris (250 BC): l'Hôtel de Ville (City Hall since 1357, King Francis I started this building in 1533, finished 1628, 1873-1892

Question 53. Will family assistance have priority?

Response: Yes, everybody understands this.

Proposition 30. Family assistance

Because all families need assistance from time to time, and the big 7.7 B family on Earth contains billions of small families, all of them will have the assistance they need – this will be the result of one country well organized and managed.

USA, Boston: 3 Dec 2009, the northeast façade of the Harvard Medical School Anno Domini 1904, founded in 1782, the graduate medical school of Harvard University, 1660 students, acceptance rate 3.7%. Harvard University: 7,200 undergraduates; 14,000 Graduates, 4,671 Faculty members; 152 Nobel laureates are members of Harvard University, 12 Schools and 2 Institutes for Advanced Studies, including Harvard School of Engineering and Applied Sciences, $32.3 billion endowment. $4.2 billion budget).

Question 54. Will abuses continue?

Response: Certainly not – it is a demanding effort, after thousands of years of all kinds of abuses, but the abuses will be gone!

Proposition 33. No abuses

33.1 - Special attention will be given by Advisors to avoid abuses and wrong interpretations of the rules. All assistants (doctors, mathematicians, CEOs, engineers and teachers) will closely monitor all activities, to avoid abuses and wrong interpretations of the rules.

33.2 - This requirement of not having abuses is demanding – but this is a general job, not only for Government, but for everybody, as part of the big family, we just don't need abuses.

33.3 - The abuse, in some places, of confiscating the land by some government bureaucrats will be eliminated – the land belongs to the people, not the government.

33.4 - The abuse, in some places, of having trains, airplanes, and others making unhealthy noises, with the government support, will be eliminated – peoples' health has always priority.

33.5 – The abuse, in some places, of having to change the clocks twice a year will be eliminated – only the normal local time zones will be used.

33.6 - If abuses are observed, they will be immediately reported to the Government, and corrected, in general, by the People Assistance Department, which will have personnel, including medical assistants, to analyze and promptly solve the abuses.

Question 55. What about commerce?

Response: Naturally there will be intense free commerce.

Proposition 34. Free commerce

34.1 - In one country, with one market, the commerce between the people on Earth will be free of taxes, tariffs, duties, etc. – plenty of opportunities for everybody.

Italy, Roma - Arco di Costantino (312, left), and Amphitheatrum Flavium (Colosseum, 80 AD, right), from Via di San Gregorio.

Question 56. Will the speech be free and responsible?

Response: Yes, the speech will be free and responsible.

34.2 - The speech will be free and responsible. It is expected not to call for war, violence, or similar destructive activities. People want peace, freedom, health, friendship and prosperity.

France, Paris: Rue Soufflot (from Panthéon, looking north-west to Jardin du Luxembourg (1612, back), and Tour Eiffel (1889, 324 m)), with the Université Paris 1 Panthéon-Sorbonne (1150, 1971, right).

Paris - A sculpture with musicians on the right side of the left outer bay on the façade of l'Opéra de Paris (1875), one of the most famous opera houses in the world, and a prestigious symbol of Paris. In interior, the ceiling area, which surrounds the chandelier, contains a new 1964 painting by Marc Chagall, which was installed on a removable frame over the original, and depicts scenes from operas by 14 composers, including, Mozart, Bizet, Verdi and Beethoven.

Question 57. Will the press be free and responsible?

Response: Yes, the press will be free and responsible – it is expected that the press will help the people.

34.3 - The press will be free and responsible. It is expected not to call for war, violence, or similar destructive activities. People want peace, freedom, health, friendship and prosperity.

Italy, 6 April 1978, Pisa, Cattedrale di Pisa (1092, striped-marble, left), Torre di Pisa (August 1173-1372, 55.86 m on the low side, 56.67 m on the high side, white-marble, 296 steps, right).

Question 58. Will some people be able to protest violently?

Response: No - people can assemble peacefully only. If some disagree with a decision, they can always inform the government, which will respond in 3 days. The discussion will continue with calm and respect, until everything is clarified.

34.4 - People can assemble peacefully only, with police for help. It is expected not to call for war, violence, or similar destructive activities. People want peace, freedom, health, friendship and prosperity.

USA, Boston Harbor (founded in 1630), in 2009: visiting tall ships from many countries, at the Boston Fish Pier (opened in 1915).

Paris - On the façade of l'Opéra de Paris (1875): a statue and the bust of Johann Sebastian Bach (1685 – 1750), one of the greatest German composers and organists, who wrote the Branderburg Concertos, the Well-Tempered Clavier, over 200 cantatas, Passions, and keyboard works. Mozart, Beethoven, Chopin, Schumann and Mendelssohn were admirers of Bach. Beethoven described him as the "Urvater der Harmonie" (the original father of harmony).

Question 59. Will everybody have a job?

Response: Yes – there will be more jobs than people.

Proposition 35. Jobs for all

35.1 - There will always be plenty of jobs at world minimum wage (assisting other people, for example), and the standard situation will be this: more jobs than available people, so people will choose the jobs they like the most.

Italy, 6 April 1978, Pisa, Palazzo della Carovana (1562-1564) now for Scuola Normale Superiore (1810, by Napoleon Bonaparte (1769-1821), 460 students, 6% admission rate, best in Italy).

Question 60. Will beggars be everywhere?

Response: No - no unemployment, no homelessness, no begging, no tipping.

35.2 - No unemployment, no homelessness, no begging – just all working harmoniously, having good houses, and helping each other.

Japan: the north side of Mt Fuji (3,776 m, 15 km south), from the south of Kawaguchiko (830 m elevation, 100 km south-west of Tokyo), near route 139 Fuji Panorama Line.

USA, 5 Feb 2016, driving in winter 30 km northwest of Boston, on Lowell Street (5 km east of Lowell), in Andover (1642, population 34,000, named after Andover (circa 955, county of Hampshire, 100 km southwest of London, 60 km south of Oxford, England, population 64,000)). The highly selective Phillips Academy Andover (1778, the oldest incorporated high school in the USA) is a College preparatory high school (grades 9-12, 1122 students).

Question 61. How can this Constitution be improved?

Response: When 66% of the voters agree.

Proposition 37. Constitution improvements

This Constitution of the World can be improved when 66% of the voters agree.

Switzerland, Geneva, the Monument (1879) for Charles II, Duke of Brunswick (30 Oct 1804 in Brunswick (Braunschweig), Germany-19 August 1873, aged 68.8 (died in Geneva at Beau Rivage Hotel), ruled the Duchy of Brunswick 1815-1830).

USA, the University of California, Berkeley (1868, named after the philosopher and mathematician Bishop George Berkeley (1685-1753), motto Fiat lux (Let there be light), 36,200 students, major public research university, 72 Nobel laureates, between the top six universities in the world, 500 ha campus), il Campanile (Sather Tower (61 bells (full concert carillon) and clock tower). 1914, 94 m, 7 floors, observation deck on the 8th floor, inspired by il Campanile (850, 1514, 1912, 99 m) di San Marco (1084), Venezia (421, Venice), Italy (900 BC)).

Question 62. What is the purpose of the people on Earth?

Response: To be healthy, to live in peace, freedom and harmony, to be prosperous, and to prepare to expand to the Moon, asteroids, Mars, etc.

Proposition 38. General ideas

38.1 - The purpose for all people on Earth is to be healthy, to live in peace, freedom and harmony, to be prosperous, and to prepare to expand to the Moon, asteroids, Mars, and other places in the Universe, which can support life.

USA, Boston: a view of the north-east part of Boston, from Cambridge, over Charles River Basin. Federal Reserve Bank Building (187 m, left), and other tall buildings in the financial district.

Question 63. Are there immediate objectives for people?

Response: Yes, reserve time for happiness, etc.:

38.2 - Important immediate objectives for everybody are:
- Reserve time for happiness.
- Use robots and automated processes, work less, and spend more time with your family.
- The weekend will be like a small vacation.
- Prevent burnout.
- Make civilized behavior and harmony everywhere an important issue.
- Eliminate stress.
- Help friends and colleagues.
- Keep everybody relaxed, calm, friendly, patient, and happy.

France: L'église de la Madeleine (or L'église Sainte-Marie-Madeleine, or La Madeleine, 1842), a Roman Catholic Church in the 8th arrondissement of Paris, designed by Napoleon in 1806.

Question 64. Is there an example about how to start this new structure of the world?

Response: Sure:

38.3 - To start this new structure of the world, one idea could be this: the first Honorific World Observer (from UN, for example) could invite 10 Presidents form big countries (like USA, China, Russia, UK, India, France, Japan, Germany, Brasil, and Egypt) to be the first 10 Advisors Level 4, starting, for example, on January 1st, 2021, for 10 months, until November 1st, 2021, when the new calm and noiseless elections will take place. The same for the 100 Advisers Level 3, and so on.

USA: California: From the Claremont Club & Spa looking north to a part of Berkeley.

Question 65. Are there books for better understanding this Constitution?

Response: Certainly:

38.4 - For better understanding and easier implementation of this Constitution, the following books, by Michael M. Dediu, are recommended:
- Our Future is Sustainable Peace and Prosperity – Moving from conflicts to harmony and peace
– Our Future Depends on Good World Educations – Moving from frail education to solid education.
– Friendly, Helpful & Smart World Management - Moving from bureaucracy to responsive world management
– If You Want Peace, Prepare for Peace! – Moving from preparation for war to preparation for peace
– World with One Country & its Ten Friendly Regions - Moving from 195 disagreeing countries, to 1 country with 10 collaborating regions
– After 10,000 Years of Conflicts, People want 10,000 Years of Harmony - Moving from continuous wars to stable peace
- The Constitution of the World – Moving from many unsustainable constitutions, to just one Constitution of the World
- World Constitution Implementation – Moving from violent changes, to smooth transition to the Constitution of the World
- It is getting truer and truer – we urgently need the World Constitution: Moving from anarchic changes, to balanced transition to the Constitution of the World
- World Constitution with Lovely Comments - Moving from many suboptimal constitutions to the much better Constitution of the World

UK: London (founded by Romans in 43, population 8.6 M), Elephant and Castle (EaC) area, near Newington Butts St., from Brook Drive looking southeast to a new tall residential building, 60 m south of Metropolitan Tabernacle (1650 Baptist church), 100 m southwest of the EaC Shopping Centre, 200 m southwest of the Elephant and Castle railroad station, and 250 m southwest of the Michael Faraday (1791-1867, physicist and chemist with many discoveries) Memorial (1961, stainless steel box-shaped building).

Question 66. For what territories is this Constitution intended?

Response: For all Earth, the space around Earth, for the Moon, Mars, asteroids, etc.

Proposition 39. Extensions

This Constitution of the World is valid not only on Earth, but also on the space around Earth, on the Moon, Mars, asteroids and any other places were the very good people on Earth will be moving in the future.

Japan: The north side of the Osaka Castle (1597, 58 m, by Toyotomi Hideyoshi, rebuilt, with a museum), 5 km southeast of Shin-Osaka.

Question 67. How long will this Constitution be working?

Response: For at least 10,000 years of harmonious living

Proposition 40. Intentions and putting into practice

40-1 - This Constitution of the World is intended for at least 10,000 years of harmonious living on the happy Earth.

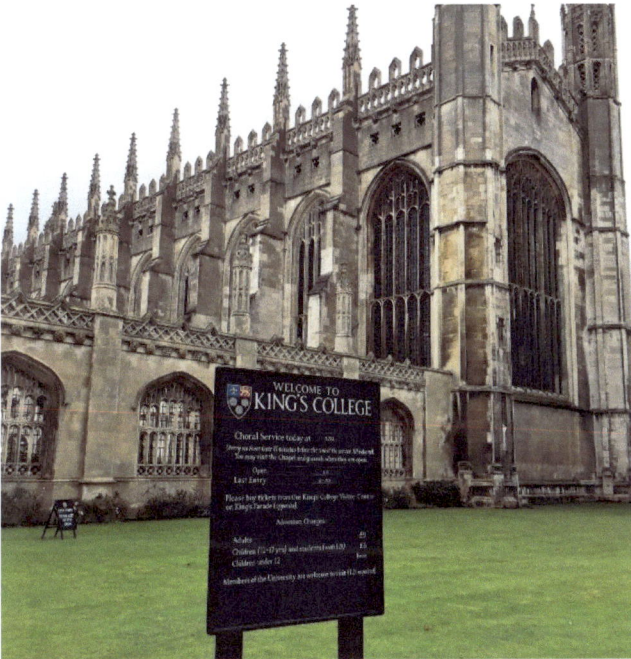

UK, Cambridge, from the entrance to King's College (1441), looking northwest to the Chapel (the south façade (center left), and the east façade (right)).

UK, London, on St Thomas St, looking southeast to the Shard (2009-2012, at London Bridge, 309 m (the tallest building in European Union), observatory at 244 m (72nd floor, 758 m^2), 95 floors, 72 habitable floors, 110,000 m^2 (11 ha) floor area, 44 elevators, architect Renzo Piano (born 1937, inspired by the London spires depicted by Canaletto (1697-1768)), 11,000 panes of glass (with a total surface area of 56,000 m^2 (5.6 ha)), post-tensioned concrete and composite floors, load-bearing pillars, tapering shape (sway tolerance 40 cm).

Question 68. When will this Constitution be ready to come into force?

Response: On 6 March 2020.

40.2 – The present Constitution of the World is ready to come into force, and to be put into practice, for the benefit of all people on Earth, on 6 March 2020, and it is ready to remain into force, and enjoyed by all people, at least until 6 March 12020.

Italy, Venezia - The south end of La Piazzetta, the south part of Piazza San Marco, with gondole, and wedding pictures of a Japanese couple.

UK, London, from the Shard (2012, 309 m, observatory at 244 m), looking west to River Thames (flowing from west (up left) to east (right down), 346 km, discharge 66 m^3/s), a railroad bridge (right down, going to Cannon Street Station), Southwalk Bridge (right center), Millennium Bridge (center right, steel suspension bridge for pedestrians), another railroad bridge (going to Blackfriars Station) just 40 m east of the Blackfriars Bridge (center up), and the last bridge before Thames turns south (left) – Waterloo Bridge.

www.ingramcontent.com/pod-product-compliance
Lightning Source LLC
Chambersburg PA
CBHW041309210326
41599CB00003B/46